December 2000

FAA COMPUTER SECURITY

Recommendations to Address Continuing Weaknesses

GAO-01-171

United States General Accounting Office
Washington, D.C. 20548

December 6, 2000

The Honorable Rodney E. Slater
The Secretary of Transportation

Dear Mr. Secretary:

In September, we testified before the Committee on Science, House of Representatives, on the Federal Aviation Administration's (FAA) computer security program.[1] In brief, we reported that FAA's agencywide computer security program has serious, pervasive problems in the following key areas:

- personnel security,
- facility physical security,
- operational systems security,
- information systems security management,
- service continuity, and
- intrusion detection.

We also noted that until FAA addresses the pervasive weaknesses in its computer security program, its critical information systems will remain at increased risk of intrusion and attack, and its aviation operations will remain at risk. These critical weaknesses need to be addressed. To assist you in bringing this about, we are making recommendations to you based on the suggestions we made in our September 2000 testimony, which is reprinted in appendix I.

We performed our work from March through September 2000, in accordance with generally accepted government auditing standards. Department of Transportation (DOT) and FAA officials provided us with comments on a draft of this report; they are discussed in the "Agency Comments" section.

Recommendations

Given the importance of a comprehensive and effective computer security program, we recommend that the Secretary of Transportation direct the FAA Administrator to complete the following actions.

---

[1]*FAA Computer Security: Actions Needed to Address Critical Weaknesses That Jeopardize Aviation Operations* (GAO/T-AIMD-00-330, September 27, 2000).

In the area of personnel security,

- actively track when reinvestigations of federal employees are due, and ensure that they occur;
- move expeditiously to complete the required background searches of contract employees;
- verify the background searches of both current and prior contract employees who performed or are performing vulnerability assessments, and update or upgrade these background searches as warranted; and
- perform vulnerability assessments of the critical systems that were worked on by foreign nationals in order to assess these systems' vulnerability to unauthorized access.

In the area of facility physical security,

- proceed quickly to complete facility assessments, perform corrective actions on any weaknesses identified during these facility assessments, and accredit these facilities.

In the area of operational systems security,

- proceed quickly to complete assessments of all operational air traffic control (ATC) systems, address any weaknesses identified during these assessments, and accredit these systems;
- complete efforts to implement and enforce a comprehensive configuration management/software change control policy;
- complete overall security guidance documents, including a security concept of operations and security standards; and
- ensure that new systems development efforts conform with policy requirements and the information systems security architecture.

In the area of information systems security management,

- complete the information systems security directives;
- fully implement and enforce all security policies; and
- complete efforts to develop and implement new information systems security training courses.

In the area of service continuity,

- assess the effects of security breaches on all systems;

- enhance existing contingency plans to address potential systems security breaches; and
- correct inadequacies in facility contingency plans.

In the area of intrusion detection,

- increase efforts to establish a fully operational Computer Security and Intrusion Response Capability that allows for the detection, analysis, and reporting of all computer systems security incidents promptly and
- ensure that all physical security incidents are reported to security personnel.

As you know, the head of a federal agency is required by 31 U.S.C. 720 to submit a written statement on the actions taken on our recommendations to the Senate Committee on Governmental Affairs and the House Committee on Government Reform not later than 60 days after the date of this report. A written statement must also be sent to the House and Senate Committees on Appropriations with the agency's first request for appropriations made more than 60 days after the date of this report.

Agency Comments

We obtained oral comments on a draft of this report from DOT and FAA officials, including representatives of the Office of the Secretary of Transportation, FAA's Chief Information Officer, FAA's Director of Information Systems Security, and FAA's Deputy Associate Administrator for Civil Aviation Security. These officials generally agreed with our recommendations and stated that they are working to implement them. In addition, these officials offered detailed comments, which we have incorporated as appropriate.

We are sending copies of this report to Senator Slade Gorton, Senator Frank R. Lautenberg, Senator Joseph I. Lieberman, Senator John D. Rockefeller IV, Senator Richard C. Shelby, Senator Fred Thompson, Representative James A. Barcia, Representative John J. Duncan, Representative Ralph M. Hall, Representative Steven Horn, Representative William O. Lipinski, Representative Constance A. Morella, Representative Martin O. Sabo, Representative F. James Sensenbrenner, Jr., Representative Jim Turner, and Representative Frank R. Wolf in their capacities as Chairmen or Ranking Minority Members of Senate and House Committees and Subcommittees.

We are also sending copies of this report to the Honorable Jane F. Garvey, Administrator of the Federal Aviation Administration, and to the Honorable Jacob J. Lew, Director of the Office of Management and Budget. Copies will also be made available to others upon request.

Should you or your staff have any questions concerning this report, please contact me at (202) 512-6408 or Linda Koontz, Director, Information Management Issues, at (202) 512-6240. We can also be reached by e-mail at *willemssenj@gao.gov* and *koontzl@gao.gov*, respectively. Major contributors to this report are identified in appendix II.

Sincerely yours,

Joel C. Willemssen
Managing Director, Information Technology Issues

United States General Accounting Office

GAO

Testimony

Before the Committee on Science, House of Representatives

For Release on Delivery
Expected at
10 a.m. EDT
Wednesday
September 27, 2000

FAA COMPUTER SECURITY

Actions Needed to Address Critical Weaknesses That Jeopardize Aviation Operations

Statement of Joel C. Willemssen
Director, Civil Agencies Information Systems
Accounting and Information Management Division

GAO
Accountability ★ Integrity ★ Reliability

GAO/T-AIMD-00-330

Mr. Chairman and Members of the Committee:

Thank you for inviting us to participate in today's hearing on the continuing challenges facing the Federal Aviation Administration (FAA) in the area of computer security. Computers and electronic data are indispensable to critical federal operations, including national defense, tax collection, import control, benefits payments, and air traffic control. However, this reliance on automated systems increases the risks of disruption of critical operations and services, fraud, and inappropriate disclosure of sensitive data. Organized attacks, such as the "Solar Sunrise" attack on Department of Defense (DOD) in early 1998, and widespread computer virus infections, such as the Melissa and ILOVEYOU viruses, illustrate our government's susceptibility to malicious computer-based actions.[1]

While complete summary data on computer security incidents is not available, it is clear that the number of such incidents is growing. The fourth annual survey conducted by the Computer Security Institute in cooperation with the Federal Bureau of Investigation (FBI) showed an increase in computer security intrusions for the third year in a row. In addition, the Defense Information Systems Agency recently reported that a total of 22,144 attacks were detected on Defense Department networks last year, up from 5,844 in 1998. Recognizing the federal government's increasing reliance on computer systems to perform its basic missions, it is imperative that agencies secure their critical computer systems and electronic data. To elevate attention to this growing problem, we designated information security as a governmentwide high-risk issue in 1997, and again in 1999.[2]

My statement today provides the final results of a review undertaken for this Committee over the past few months in which we were asked to assess FAA's progress in implementing its overall computer security program, including the status of weaknesses we identified in previous

---

[1] Critical Infrastructure Protection: "ILOVEYOU" Computer Virus Highlights Need for Improved Alert and Coordination Capabilities (GAO/T-AIMD-00-181, May 18, 2000). Information Security: "ILOVEYOU" Computer Virus Emphasizes Critical Need for Agency and Governmentwide Improvements (GAO/T-AIMD-00-171, May 10, 2000). Information Security: The Melissa Computer Virus Demonstrates Urgent Need for Stronger Protection Over Systems and Sensitive Data (GAO/T-AIMD-99-146, April 15, 1999).

[2] High-Risk Series: Information Management and Technology (GAO/HR-97-09, February 1997) and High-Risk Series: An Update (GAO/HR-99-1, January 1999).

reports.[3] After providing background information on FAA's air traffic control system and its reliance on integrated computer systems, I would like to discuss (1) FAA's history of computer security weaknesses, (2) the adequacy of FAA's efforts to prevent unauthorized access to data—specifically focusing on personnel security, facilities' physical security, systems security, security program planning and management, and service continuity, and (3) the effectiveness of processes implemented by the agency for detecting, responding to, and reporting anomalies and computer misuse. An overview of our objectives, scope, and methodology is provided in appendix I.

In brief, FAA's agencywide computer security program has serious and pervasive problems. For example,

- In the area of personnel security, FAA appears to perform appropriate background searches for federal employees, but many Top Secret reinvestigations of senior personnel are past due—some by over 5 years. FAA is also working to complete background searches on thousands of its contractor employees, but much work remains to be done;

- In the area of facilities' physical security, FAA is making progress in assessing its facilities, but the agency has identified significant weaknesses, and numerous air traffic control (ATC) facilities have yet to be assessed and accredited as secure, in compliance with FAA's policy;

- FAA does not know how vulnerable the majority of its operational ATC systems are and cannot adequately protect them until it performs the appropriate risk assessments and addresses identified weaknesses. Further, FAA has not always acted quickly to implement corrective actions for the systems that have undergone risk assessments and penetration testing;

- FAA has established an information systems security management structure, but does not yet have a comprehensive security program in place;

- FAA's efforts to ensure service continuity are limited; and

---

[3] Air Traffic Control: Weak Computer Security Practices Jeopardize Flight Safety (GAO/AIMD-98-155, May 18, 1998), Computer Security: FAA Needs to Improve Controls Over Use of Foreign Nationals to Remediate and Review Software (GAO/AIMD-00-55, December 23, 1999), and Computer Security: FAA Is Addressing Personnel Weaknesses, But Further Action Is Required (GAO/AIMD-00-169, May 31, 2000).

Page 3   GAO/T-AIMD-00-330 FAA Computer Security

- FAA has not yet fully implemented an intrusion detection capability that will enable it to quickly detect and respond to malicious intrusions.

  Over the last 3 years, we have conducted four detailed reviews of FAA's computer security program and made 22 recommendations to help improve critical weaknesses we identified.[4] The agency has made some progress in addressing these recommendations, but has not yet fully implemented most of them. Until FAA addresses the pervasive weaknesses in its computer security program, its critical information systems will remain at increased risk of intrusion and attack, and its aviation operations will remain at risk.

Background

FAA's mission is to ensure safe, orderly, and efficient air travel in the national airspace system (NAS). FAA's ability to fulfill this mission depends on the adequacy and reliability of its ATC system, a vast network of computer hardware, software, and communications equipment.

Faced with rapidly growing air traffic volumes and aging air traffic equipment, in 1981 FAA initiated an ambitious ATC modernization program. This program includes the acquisition of a vast network of radar and automated data processing, navigation, and communications equipment in addition to new facilities and support equipment. The modernization is expected to cost $40 billion through fiscal year 2004.[5]

ATC Facilities

Automated information processing and display, communication, navigation, surveillance, and weather resources permit air traffic controllers to view key information, such as aircraft location,

aircraft flight plans, and prevailing weather conditions, and to communicate with pilots. These resources reside at, or are associated with, several types of ATC facilities—air traffic control towers, terminal radar approach control (TRACON) facilities, air route traffic control centers (en route centers), flight service stations, and the Air Traffic Control System Command Center (ATCSCC). These facilities' ATC functions are described below.

---

[4]GAO/AIMD-98-155, May 18, 1998; GAO/AIMD-00-55, December 23, 1999; GAO/AIMD-00-169, May 31, 2000; and *FAA Computer Security: Concerns Remain Due to Personnel and Other Continuing Weaknesses* (GAO/AIMD-00-252, August 16, 2000).

[5]The total cost of modernization includes appropriations for all actual and projected facilities and equipment from fiscal year 1982 through fiscal 2004 for projects in FAA's financial plan.

- Airport towers control aircraft on the ground and before landing and after take-off when they are within about 5 nautical miles of the airport, and up to 3,000 feet above the airport.

- Approximately 180 TRACONs sequence and separate aircraft as they approach and leave busy airports, beginning about 5 nautical miles and ending about 50 nautical miles from the airport, and generally up to 10,000 feet above the airport, where en route centers' control begins.

- Twenty en route centers control planes over the continental United States in transit and during approaches to some airports. Each en route center handles a different region of airspace, passing control from one to another as respective borders are reached until the aircraft reaches TRACON airspace. En route center controlled airspace usually extends above 18,000 feet for commercial aircraft. En route centers also handle lower altitudes when dealing directly with a tower, or when agreed upon with a TRACON.

- Two en route centers--Oakland and New York--also control aircraft over the ocean. Controlling aircraft over oceans is radically different from controlling aircraft over land because radar surveillance only extends 175 to 225 miles offshore. Beyond the radars' sight, controllers must rely on periodic radio communications through a third party—Aeronautical Radio Incorporated (ARINC), a private organization funded by the airlines and FAA to operate radio stations—to determine aircraft locations.

- About 90 flight service stations provide pre-flight and in-flight services, such as flight plan filing and weather report updates, primarily for general aviation aircraft.

- Located in Herndon, Virginia, the ATCSCC is used to manage the flow of air traffic within the continental United States. This facility regulates air traffic when weather, equipment, runway closures, or other impacting conditions place stress on the NAS. In these instances, Traffic Management Specialists at the ATCSCC take action to modify traffic demands in order to remain within system capacity.

See figure 1 for a visual summary of air traffic control over the continental United States and oceans.

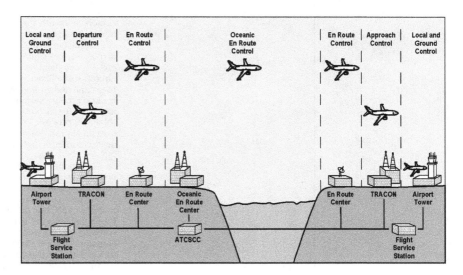

Figure 1: Summary of Air Traffic Control Over the Continental United States and Oceans

ATC Infrastructure Is a Complex Integrated System of Systems

FAA information systems, which include those supporting the NAS as well as mission support systems, are very large, highly automated, and support both public and private interests. FAA systems supporting the NAS process a wide range of data—including radar, weather, flight plans, surveillance, navigation/landing guidance, traffic management, air-to-ground, voice, network management, and other information—that is required to support the FAA mission. Many FAA mission support systems provide information such as aircraft certification, inspection, flight standards, and regulatory information to support the operational mission of safe aircraft traffic control.

The ability of FAA's systems to interoperate, both within and across facilities, as one integrated system-of-systems is essential to ATC operations.[6] Each type of facility highlighted in the previous section contains numerous interrelated systems. For example, the en route centers alone rely on over 50 systems to perform mission-critical information processing and display, navigation, surveillance, communications, and weather functions. These include the systems that display aircraft situation data for air traffic controllers, the system that collects and displays data from various weather sources, radars for aircraft surveillance, radars for wind and precipitation detection, ground-to-ground and ground-to-air communications systems, and systems to backup primary systems. In addition, systems from different facilities also interact with each other so that together they can successfully execute the total ATC process. For example, controllers' displays currently integrate data on aircraft position from surveillance radars with data on flight destination from flight planning data systems.

As FAA continues to modernize its ATC systems, computer security will become even more critical. Newer systems use digital computer networking and telecommunications technologies that can expose the NAS to new vulnerabilities and risks that must be assessed and mitigated to ensure adequate protection. New vulnerabilities also result from the FAA's increasing reliance upon commercially available hardware and software, as well as growing interconnectivity among computer and communication systems. Increasing interconnection increases the extent to which the system becomes vulnerable to intruders who may severely disrupt operations, obtain sensitive information, or manipulate data to commit fraud.

FAA Has a History of Computer Security Problems

FAA has a history of computer security weaknesses in a number of areas, including its physical security management at facilities that house air traffic control (ATC) systems, systems security for both operational and future systems, management structure for implementing security policies, and personnel security. Over the last 3 years, we have made 22 recommendations to FAA to address these security weaknesses.[7]

---

[6]Interoperability is the ability of disparate systems to work together efficiently and effectively over a network.

[7]GAO/AIMD-98-155, May 18, 1998; GAO/AIMD-00-55, December 23, 1999; and GAO/AIMD-00-169, May 31, 2000.

In May 1998, we reported that FAA had significant weaknesses in every area of computer security that we reviewed.[8] Specifically, we noted:

- Physical security management and controls at facilities that house ATC systems were ineffective;

- Systems security—for both operational and future systems—were ineffective, rendering systems vulnerable; and

- FAA's management structure for implementing and enforcing computer security policy was ineffective.

For example, known physical security weaknesses at one ATC facility included unauthorized personnel being granted unescorted access to restricted areas. Further, FAA did not know about vulnerabilities at 187 other facilities because security controls had not been assessed since 1993. In the area of systems security, FAA was in violation of its own policy and had performed the necessary analysis to determine system threats, vulnerabilities, and safeguards on only 3 of its 90 operational ATC computer systems. FAA was likewise not effectively managing the security of future ATC systems modernization efforts because it did not consistently include well-defined security requirements in its specifications, as its policy mandates. Further, FAA's overall management structure and implementation of policy for ATC computer security was not effective. Responsibilities were dispersed among three entities within the agency, all of which were remiss in their ATC security duties.

More recently, we evaluated FAA's status on another element of computer security—personnel security—in our December 1999 report.[9] That report disclosed that FAA was not following its own personnel security practices and, thus, had increased the risk that inappropriate individuals may have gained access to its facilities, information, or resources. FAA's policy requires system owners and users to prepare risk assessments for all contractor tasks, and to conduct background investigations of all contract employees in high-risk positions; it requires less thorough background checks for moderate- and low-risk positions. FAA did not, however, perform all required risk assessments, and was unaware of whether background searches had been performed on all contract employees. We found instances in which background searches were not performed—

---

[8]GAO/AIMD-98-155, May 18, 1998.

[9]GAO/AIMD-00-55, December 23, 1999.

including on 36 mainland Chinese nationals who reviewed the computer source code of eight mission-critical systems as part of FAA's effort to ensure Year 2000 readiness. By again not following its own policies, FAA increased the exposure of its systems to intrusion and malicious attack.

In our reports, we made recommendations to, among other things, address weaknesses in

- physical security—by inspecting all ATC facilities that had not been recently inspected, correcting any identified weaknesses, and accrediting these facilities;[10]

- operational ATC systems security—by assessing, certifying, and accrediting[11] all systems by April 30, 1999, and at least every 3 years thereafter, as required by federal policy;

- future ATC systems security—by including well-formulated security requirements in the specifications for all new ATC systems;

- security management—by developing an effective CIO management structure for implementing and enforcing computer security policy; and

- personnel security—by tightening controls over contract employees by ensuring that appropriate background searches are performed.

Ineffective Personnel Security Management Places Operational ATC Systems at Risk

Effective personnel security is essential to protecting critical assets—including facilities, information, and resources. FAA's personnel security policy requires that (1) the level of risk associated with each federal and contractor employee position be assessed, and (2) that background searches—checks or investigations—be conducted for each employee, with the type of search depending on the level of risk associated with the individual's position. For federal employees, the agency requires a minimum of a National Agency Check and Inquiries (NACI) for all low- and moderate-risk positions. A NACI entails checking prior and current residences, previous employment, references, law enforcement records,

---

[10]At the time of our review, FAA's policy required that ATC facilities be inspected to determine if they met physical security standards. This inspection then served as the basis for accrediting a facility—concluding that it is secure.

[11]System certification is the technical evaluation that is conducted to verify that FAA systems comply with security requirements. Certification results are one factor management considers in deciding whether to accredit systems. Accreditation is the formal declaration that the appropriate security safeguards have been properly implemented and that the residual risk is acceptable.

and fingerprints. Higher risk positions warrant more thorough Background Investigations (BI). For contractor employees, a minimum of a fingerprint check is required for low-risk positions, with a NACI required for medium-risk positions, and a BI for high-risk positions.

Background Searches for Federal Employees In Headquarters Appear to Be Complete, However Many Required Reinvestigations Have Not Been Performed

Agency reports show that FAA has largely complied with its policy of conducting investigations for the vast majority of its federal employees. According to its records, as of June 8, 2000, FAA had completed background searches for 99 percent (47,585) of its approximately 48,000 employees.[12] According to FAA records, the agency conducted NACI or BI searches on 97 percent of its 47,585 federal employees who received background searches.[13] To determine whether the agency had performed the appropriate type of background search for its federal employees, we selected a statistically valid sample of the 3,702 federal employees located at FAA headquarters and reviewed documentation contained within personnel and/or security files maintained by FAA. For each of the individuals in our sample, the type of background search appeared appropriate based on the individual's responsibilities. Because we selected a statistical sample, the results are projectable to the larger population of FAA federal employees located at headquarters.[14]

While the type of searches FAA conducted appear appropriate, many of them are out of date. Federal regulations and FAA policy require individuals with Top Secret clearances to have a reinvestigation every 5 years.[15] However, many FAA reinvestigations were not performed. Of 350 headquarters employees with Top Secret clearances, 75 (21 percent) were overdue for reinvestigations as of September 5, 2000, with one individual's last investigation having occurred in 1973. Figure 2 shows the number of individuals whose reinvestigations were past due and the last date an investigation was performed for these individuals.

---

[12] We did not verify the accuracy of FAA's data for these 48,000 employees.

[13] FAA reported that there were a number of reasons that the remaining 1 percent did not have background searches, including cases in which individuals were in temporary positions, and thus did not require searches, and cases in which individuals' paperwork was still being processed.

[14] These results are projectable with an 80 percent confidence level.

[15] The federal personnel security system was established after World War II to support the system for classifying information and to investigate the loyalty of federal employees. Over the years, several regulations and directives have been issued to meet these objectives. In August 1995, the President signed Executive Order 12968, which established a uniform federal personnel security program for all government employees with access to classified information. In March 1997, the President approved the investigative standards for background investigations, which, among other topics, detail the requirements for reinvestigations.

Figure 2: Number of Individuals With Top Secret Clearance Reinvestigations Past Due

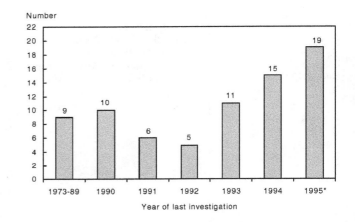

Number

*Individuals with investigation dates later than September 5, 1995, were not included in this analysis.

Source: GAO analysis of FAA data

Of these 75 individuals, 39 (52 percent) hold senior management positions within the FAA such as program directors, Assistant Administrators, and Associate Administrators. Twelve (31 percent) of these 39 individuals' investigations were over 5 years past due. When asked why these reinvestigations had not been performed, an agency official explained that this was not something that the security office was actively tracking. FAA needs to actively track when reinvestigations are due, and ensure that these reinvestigations occur. Until it does so, FAA faces an increased risk that inappropriate individuals could gain access to critical information.

In commenting on a draft of this statement on September 25, 2000, FAA officials stated that 66 reinvestigations are currently past due. Of these, two are no longer required because the individuals plan to retire, and the rest are being processed.

Page 11   GAO/T-AIMD-00-330 FAA Computer Security

FAA Has Not Completed Required Background Searches of Contract Employees, Increasing the Likelihood of Inappropriate Access Being Gained

While FAA appears to have performed background checks on the majority of its federal employees, the same is not true of its many thousands of contract employees. In order to perform background searches on contract employees, FAA contracting officers must (1) perform a security review of all contracts and purchase orders, in coordination with the agency's security office, to determine whether they contain any sensitive work elements, (2) on those contracts with sensitive work, identify positions that require background searches (via a position-specific risk assessment form), and (3) have all of the contract employees in these positions provide completed background forms which FAA then submits to the Office of Personnel Management (OPM) or the Federal Bureau of Investigation. These agencies are expected to take from 1 week to 4 months to perform the background searches, depending on the complexity of the review.

In response to our prior reports, FAA has been working to address shortcomings in these activities.[16] On September 25, 2000, FAA officials stated that only 3,370 of the agency's 28,000 existing contracts and purchase orders required security reviews, and that these reviews had been completed. Officials further explained that these reviews resulted in the identification of approximately 14,400 people who require background searches, and estimated that of these, about 8,000 have been completed, about 2,800 are pending, and about 3,600 background searches have not yet been initiated.

Because the process of obtaining background searches is complicated and involves many different individuals—ranging from the contract employee to the contracting officer, to the security office, to the investigating agency, it will likely take a long time to complete all required background searches. Nevertheless, FAA needs to move expeditiously to complete these required background searches. Until it does so, contract employees who have not received the appropriate background checks will continue to have access to FAA's facilities, information, and/or resources.

---

[16] GAO/AIMD-00-55, December 23, 1999; GAO/AIMD-00-169, May 31, 2000; GAO/AIMD-00-252, August 16, 2000.

Contractors Who Performed Penetration Tests on Critical FAA Systems Did Not Have Adequate Background Searches

Perhaps some of the most highly sensitive work at FAA involves its recent efforts to assess key systems' security vulnerabilities. Over the last 2 years, FAA contractors have completed five system vulnerability assessments and initiated two more. These assessments often involve attempting to penetrate key NAS systems in a test environment. The completed assessments identify vulnerabilities in FAA's systems, and the individuals who performed these assessments identify large amounts of detailed information on how to access and exploit system vulnerabilities. FAA has labeled all of these assessments as "Sensitive Security Information" and instituted limitations on who is able to review them.

Despite the sensitivity of these vulnerability assessments, only 2 of the 21 contractor employees who worked, or are working, on them meet FAA requirements for background searches on individuals doing high-risk work. As noted earlier, FAA's personnel security policy requires it to perform BIs on contract employees in high-risk positions. According to the policy, this investigation should take place before the individual begins work, but at a minimum, the individual's background forms must be filed with FAA's security organization before work can begin. In cases in which a contract employee already has had a background search, FAA requires that this information be provided to its security organization. The security organization is expected to verify the information, and update it or upgrade it, if necessary, and enter all information on contract employees' background searches in FAA's Investigation Tracking System (ITS).

All of the 21 contractor employees who worked, or are working, on vulnerability assessments were reported by their contractors to have undergone some form of background check. However, only two individuals meet FAA's requirements for high-risk positions in that they had undergone sufficiently rigorous background investigations, and that this information was verified and entered into ITS. Of the remaining 19 contract employees, 14 were not listed in the ITS database. An FAA official acknowledged that these individuals did not provide their background information to the security organization, and therefore the security organization did not verify their reported prior background searches, and update or upgrade these searches, if warranted. The remaining 5 individuals were identified in the database; however, four had undergone fingerprint checks and one had undergone a National Agency Check (NAC). Neither type of check is sufficient under FAA's guidelines for high-risk positions. As a result, FAA allowed and is continuing to allow contractors to undertake sensitive assessments of the weaknesses in its systems without sufficient assurance that the individuals performing the assessments are reliable and trustworthy.

An FAA official noted that several of these vulnerability assessments were done prior to our December 1999[17] report highlighting shortcomings in the agency's process for obtaining contractors' background searches, and that the agency is now working to obtain the required background searches on current contracts. However, FAA needs to verify both current and prior contract employees' background searches, and update or upgrade these investigations as warranted. Until it does so, FAA will continue to increase the risk that untrustworthy individuals have gained, or will gain, access to sensitive information on critical systems' vulnerabilities.

After 9 Months, Sufficient Background Searches of Foreign Nationals Involved in Key Year 2000 Activities Have Still Not Been Performed, Extent of Exposure Unknown

In response to our December 1999 recommendations to assess the potential exposure of systems that had been worked on by foreign nationals, FAA reported that it had performed security reviews of critical systems and retroactive security checks on contractor personnel, including foreign nationals, and did not have any negative findings. However, neither the security reviews nor the retroactive background checks were sufficient. FAA was unable to provide evidence that thorough security reviews were performed and simply noted that the risk of potential system compromise was low based on background checks performed. However, FAA security officials reported that only name checks had been performed by the Central Intelligence Agency (CIA) for foreign national employees.[18] These officials acknowledged that CIA name checks are not a sufficient background search for FAA work, but stated that they believe they were legally unable to do a more thorough check because the employees were no longer working on the contract. FAA officials also told us that they plan to further assess these systems' exposure as part of the system risk assessments. FAA needs to do so. Until these security reviews are completed, the full extent of these systems' potential vulnerability to unauthorized access will remain unknown.

---

[17]GAO/AIMD-00-55, December 23, 1999.

[18]A "name check" entails checking the individual's name against a database of suspected terrorists to determine if the individual is suspected of criminal activity.

FAA Is Making Progress on Facilities' Physical Security, Yet Vulnerabilities Exist and Much Work Remains To Be Done

Physical access controls are critical to ensuring the safety and security of facilities and the people and systems in these facilities. These controls typically restrict the entry and exit of personnel from an area, such as an office building, suite, data center, or room containing a network server. They also protect the wiring used to connect system elements, the electric power service, the air conditioning and heating plant, telephone and data lines, backup media and source documents, and any other elements required for a system's operation. Physical security controls can include controlled areas, barriers that isolate each area, entry points in the barriers, and screening measures at each of the entry points. In addition, staff members who work in a restricted area serve an important role in providing physical security, as they can be trained to challenge people they do not recognize.

In May 1998, we reported that physical security management and controls at facilities that house ATC were ineffective in that FAA had failed to inspect all facilities, implement corrective measures, and then accredit these facilities.[19] Since that time, FAA reported that it inspected and accredited 297 facilities. However, in March 1999, FAA issued a more rigorous policy governing the accreditation of its facilities. The new policy requires that in order to obtain accreditation, a facility must undergo (1) a more stringent, detailed assessment, (2) implementation of corrective actions, and (3) a follow-up inspection to ensure that corrective actions were implemented. The new policy also dictates that even after accreditation, a facility will be regularly inspected to ensure that it still meets accreditation requirements. Accordingly, FAA officials noted that all facilities that had been inspected and accredited under the prior policy would need to be assessed and re-accredited under the revised policy.

According to FAA officials, as of August 8, 2000, 237 staffed ATC facilities[20] have been assessed,[21] 42 have had follow-up inspections, and 9 have been accredited under the new policy.

In performing its facility risk assessments, FAA identified numerous weaknesses that must be addressed before the facilities can be accredited.

---

[19]GAO/AIMD-98-155, May 18, 1998.

[20]ATC facilities include towers, terminal radar approach control facilities, en route centers, center approach control facilities, radar approach control facilities, flight service stations, and radar sites.

[21] While FAA officials determined that the total number of ATC facilities that have not yet been assessed is too sensitive to release publicly, they noted that the 237 facilities that have been assessed include all of the larger ATC facilities.

While many of these weaknesses are too sensitive to discuss in a public forum, others included

- facilities with an inadequate Facility Security Plan, a structured site-specific physical security plan that is used by facility managers to implement adequate physical security protective measures,

- facilities whose staff had not had annual security education and awareness briefings,

- facilities with contractor staff who had not had the required background checks conducted, and

- facilities with inadequate contingency plans.

In performing its follow-up inspections, FAA determined that many corrective actions have not yet been implemented. As of August 15, 2000, 61 staffed ATC facilities required follow-up inspections and FAA had conducted inspections for 33 (54 percent) of these facilities, as well as an additional 9 facilities whose inspections were not yet due. Four of these 42 inspections resulted in facilities being accredited, while 38 inspections showed that significant weaknesses still remained.

As for its future plans, FAA officials expect to complete all of the facility assessments by the end of 2002, and has set a goal of accrediting 66 facilities by September 30, 2000[22] and the remaining facilities by 2005. FAA needs to proceed quickly to complete its facility assessments, corrective actions, and accreditations. Until it does so, FAA will continue to lack assurance that it can effectively prevent the loss or damage of its property, injury of its employees, and compromise of its ability to perform critical aviation functions.

In commenting on a draft of this statement, FAA officials told us that as of September 22, 2000, 295 staffed ATC facilities had now been assessed, 87 have had follow-up inspections, and 48 have been accredited.

---

[22]FAA's goal of accrediting 66 facilities includes both ATC and non-ATC facilities, such as office buildings.

Operational Systems Security Is Ineffective; Efforts to Build Security Into Future Systems Are Ongoing

To ensure that its operational systems are adequately protected, FAA requires that its systems undergo (1) risk assessments to identify and rank weaknesses, (2) correction of these weaknesses, and then (3) certification and accreditation. FAA policy also requires system re-certification and re-accreditation every 3 years or sooner, if there is a major system or environmental change that impacts the security of the system. Major changes include adding new or additional connectivity to other systems, implementing major hardware or software changes, or when a significant security breach has occurred. Additionally, FAA requires system owners to obtain proper approvals for all software changes and to build security in to all new system development efforts.

More Extensive Effort Required to Protect Operational Systems From Unauthorized Access

FAA has made little progress on our 1998 recommendation to assess, certify, and accredit all ATC systems by April 1999. Agency officials acknowledge that much work remains to be done. Of its approximately 90 operational ATC systems, the agency has performed risk assessments for 37[23] systems, certified 7 systems, and accredited 6 systems.[24]

The system risk assessments showed that significant weaknesses exist, potentially exposing the systems to unauthorized access. Such weaknesses include, but are not limited to the following:

- User identification and/or passwords are not always required and, in some instances, group user identification and/or passwords are allowed resulting in the lack of user accountability;

- Users are not always authenticated when access is gained through an external network;

- Some software contains known, exploitable bugs, and tracking of publicized software product vulnerabilities is inadequate;

---

[23]FAA officials reported that they have completed comprehensive risk assessments on 8 operational systems and that another 12 systems' assessments have been initiated but have not yet been completed. FAA also performed more limited risk assessments on 17 other operational systems, but agency officials acknowledged that these systems will need to undergo comprehensive risk assessments prior to certification and accreditation.

[24] In August 2000, we reported that eight systems had received both certification and accreditation; however, since then FAA officials reported that two of these systems had undergone significant changes requiring the risk assessments to be redone which according to FAA policy, invalidates any previous certification and accreditation.

- System owners are not always aware of unauthorized hardware connections and software installations;

- Virus control tools and procedures are not consistently applied;

- Firewalls do not always restrict remote users from executing some programs; and

- Some system and user activities are insufficiently monitored and reported.

In response to FAA comments on a draft of this statement, we deleted additional examples of weaknesses because agency officials stated that these examples were too sensitive to discuss in this public forum.

In addition to its risk assessments, FAA has also conducted penetration tests on several of its systems (often in a simulated environment) to identify weaknesses that could allow the systems to be compromised by both internal and external intruders. Penetration tests involve testing system access controls—such as passwords, dial-up access, and firewalls—to see if unauthorized users can gain access to sensitive and critical agency data.

FAA's system penetration tests identified significant vulnerabilities, including many that were basic and well known, such as weak or nonexistent passwords, failure to apply system patches or upgrade systems to the latest software release, poorly configured firewalls and routers that allowed excess connectivity, and inadequate intrusion detection or monitoring. Due to the sensitivity of the penetration test results, we are unable to provide further detail in this public forum.

Although the weaknesses FAA identified in its systems risk assessments and penetration tests are serious, FAA has not consistently implemented corrective actions in a timely manner. Of three ATC systems that had undergone risk assessments and penetration tests over a year ago, FAA has implemented 9 of 10 corrective actions on one system, but has yet to fully implement any of the recommended corrective actions on the other two systems. In most of these cases, a timeframe for completion has yet to be determined and, in some cases, the responsible party has yet to be identified. These weaknesses are significant and if left unresolved could potentially be exploited to gain access to these systems. Illustrating this, one year after the completion of a penetration test, the contractor team was able to successfully penetrate a system for a second time because corrective actions had not yet been implemented. Until the agency implements identified corrective actions, its systems will remain vulnerable.

Concerns also remain on most of the six systems FAA has accredited to date. Specifically, because five of these systems lacked key documents required for accreditation, they were granted interim 1-year accreditations—an action not covered in FAA's security policy. These 1-year interim accreditations expire in September 2000, therefore, all issues must be addressed and final accreditation must be completed. As of August 2000, many of these issues—including completion of risk assessments, security plans, or security testing—were still pending.

Because FAA has made little progress in assessing its operational systems, the agency does not know how vulnerable many of its systems are and has little basis for determining what protective measures are required. In addition, FAA's failure to implement needed corrective actions increases the agency's vulnerability to unauthorized attacks as noted above by the contractor team's second successful penetration of a key system. FAA needs to proceed quickly to complete its efforts to assess all operational ATC systems, address any weaknesses identified during these assessments, and accredit these systems. Until it does so, it continues to run the risk that intruders will gain access and exploit the systems' weaknesses.

Software Changes Being Made Without Proper Approval

Another aspect of protecting operational systems is ensuring that all modifications to the systems and software are approved. Without proper software change controls, there are risks that security features could be inadvertently or deliberately omitted or rendered inoperable, processing irregularities could occur, or malicious code could be introduced. We recently reported that across the government, software change control policies for federal information systems were inadequate.[25]

While FAA has historically had a change control board for the NAS, the agency recently recognized the need to standardize its approach to configuration management throughout the agency. To do so, it established the NAS Configuration Management and Evaluation Staff organization. This organization has developed a program plan that outlines its goals with proposed timeframes and issued a new configuration management policy. However, the supporting procedures which will provide detail on the required actions are still in draft form, and these procedures do not include security considerations. The CIO's office is currently drafting security procedures for incorporation into the configuration management

---

[25] *Information Security: Controls Over Software Changes at Federal Agencies*, (GAO/AIMD-00-151R, May 4, 2000).

Page 19   GAO/T-AIMD-00-330 FAA Computer Security

process. These procedures will address key issues, such as the preparation of risk assessments during the pre-development phase to ensure that security risks, if any, are being mitigated to an acceptable level.[26]

Agency officials acknowledged that because there is currently no quality assurance or oversight function in place to enforce the policy, some systems are being modified without receiving proper approval. They also acknowledged that they are unsure of the extent of the problem. FAA needs to fully implement and enforce a comprehensive configuration management/software change control policy. Until it does so, employees may continue to modify systems without proper approval, potentially resulting in inadequate documentation of changes and insufficient consideration of security issues. Further, because of the interconnectivity of the NAS, the failure to adequately document changes and address security issues in one system could increase the overall vulnerability of other systems and the NAS as a whole.

Security Requirements Generally Being Considered During New Systems Design, But More Guidance and Enforcement Are Needed

Essential computer security measures can be provided most effectively and cost efficiently if they are addressed during systems design. Retrofitting security features into an operational system is far more expensive and often less effective. Sound overall security guidance—including a security architecture, security concept of operations, and security standards—is needed to ensure that well formulated security requirements are included in new systems.

In May 1998, we reported that FAA had no security architecture, security concept of operations, or security standards and that, as a result, implementation of security requirements across development efforts was sporadic and ad hoc.[27] We also reported that, of six ATC development efforts reviewed, four had security requirements, but only two of the four had security requirements based on a risk assessment. We recommended that the agency develop and implement a security architecture, security concept of operations and security standards, and ensure that specifications for all new ATC systems include security requirements based on detailed risk assessments.

---

[26]Despite the lack of configuration management security procedures, FAA has identified minimum security criteria for systems in its Information System Security Architecture, Version 1.0 (June 30, 2000) and the Telecommunications Security Risk Management Plan (January 31, 1998).

[27]GAO/AIMD-98-155, May 18, 1998.

Since that time, FAA has made progress in developing overall security guidance and in attempting to build security into new systems, but more remains to be done. In June 2000, FAA issued version 1.0 of its security architecture, but it has not yet developed a security concept of operations or security standards. As for implementing security requirements on new development efforts, we reviewed three systems currently under development and found that progress was mixed. FAA had prepared risk assessments for all three systems, and two of the three systems had either identified or implemented security requirements based on the risk assessment, and had tested or were testing these security requirements. However, for the third system, there was no evidence that needed security features had been included in technical specifications for the system or that security testing had occurred or was underway. As a result, FAA is not consistently ensuring that security features are being incorporated and that these features will adequately mitigate security risks.

FAA needs to complete its overall security guidance documents, including a security concept of operations and security standards, and ensure that new systems development efforts conform with the current policy's requirements as well as the security architecture. Until it does so, there remains the risk that new system development efforts will not effectively address security issues.

FAA Established a CIO Management Structure for Overseeing Information Systems Security, But Has Not Yet Implemented a Comprehensive Security Program

Organizations need a management framework and effective policy implementation to manage security risks.[28] In May 1998, we reported that FAA's management structure and policy implementation for ATC computer security was ineffective because the organizations responsible for different aspects of security had failed to perform their duties. We recommended that FAA establish an effective management structure—similar to the CIO management structure outlined in the Clinger-Cohen Act—for developing, implementing, and enforcing computer security policy.

In 1999, FAA restructured its CIO position to report directly to the Administrator and tasked the CIO with the responsibility for establishing and overseeing the agency's information security program, among other activities. The CIO's office coordinates with other FAA organizations that are responsible for different aspects of computer security, including the

---

[28]We have highlighted such management practices in *Executive Guide: Information Security Management—Learning from Leading Organizations* (GAO/AIMD-98-68, May 1998) and *Information Security Risk Assessment: Practices of Leading Organizations* (GAO/AIMD-00-33, November 1999).

Page 21   GAO/T-AIMD-00-330 FAA Computer Security

Office of Civil Aviation Security, which is responsible for physical and personnel security policies, and the individual lines of business, which are responsible for implementing security policies.

While FAA has made improvements in its computer security management structure, it has not yet implemented a comprehensive information security program. In recent months, the CIO has issued version 1.0 of its information systems security architecture, and an information systems security program management plan, which formalize the agency's information systems security management structure and future plans. Additionally, in June 2000, FAA issued an updated information systems security policy. However, this new policy primarily focuses on roles and responsibilities of various groups within FAA and does not contain the procedures to be followed by the lines of business to achieve policy compliance. The CIO plans to develop these procedures, referred to as implementation directives; but could not estimate when these directives would be available. Until these directives are completed, the various lines of business responsible for policy implementation may or may not be in compliance with the agency's policy. In addition, since there is currently no enforcement or reporting mechanism in place to ensure that the various organizations are performing their assigned objectives/tasks, the CIO is unable to evaluate the policy's effectiveness in ensuring computer security.

In addition to the information systems security policy, FAA's personnel and physical security policies play an important role in protecting the agency's systems and the facilities that house them. However, as noted earlier, FAA is still not in full compliance with either of these policies. Specifically, FAA has not yet completed the required background searches for all contractor personnel, including foreign nationals, and it has not yet inspected and accredited all of its ATC facilities.

In order to establish a comprehensive and effective computer security program, FAA needs to complete its information system security directives and fully implement and enforce all security policies. Until it does so, the agency and its information and resources will remain at risk.

FAA Has Not Fully Implemented a Security Awareness and Training Program

The Computer Security Act of 1987 mandates training in security awareness and accepted security practices for "all employees who are involved with the management, use, or operation of each federal computer system within or under the supervision of that agency."[29] Awareness, a prerequisite to training, is intended to focus attention on security. Awareness programs generally provide a baseline of security knowledge for all users, regardless of job duties or position. An example of an awareness campaign would be the displaying of posters reminding users not to share passwords. Training is geared to understanding the security aspects of the particular IT systems and applications that the individual uses, such as understanding the features of the local area network to which they are connected.

FAA's recent facility and systems risk assessments frequently cited the lack of security awareness and training as a significant issue. While FAA officials determined that the specific number of facilities and systems that cited this problem is too sensitive to discuss in a public forum, a substantial number of facilities noted that annual security awareness briefings had not been conducted and several system assessments stated that system administrators had received minimal, if any, training and, as a result, were unaware of system weaknesses and how easily these weaknesses could be exploited.

Without adequate security awareness and training programs, security lapses can occur. We encountered several during the course of our review. In one instance, we were able to access a key FAA policy on the Internet despite the fact that the policy was labeled "For Official Use Only" and not supposed to be released to foreign nationals without the express written consent of FAA's security office. In addition, FAA personnel e-mailed us sensitive information, including employees' social security numbers, over the Internet.

FAA's CIO is now working to improve the agency's information systems security awareness and training programs. The CIO distributed a videotaped ISS awareness briefing, and plans to develop a web site that would enable individuals to easily obtain security awareness and training information. FAA also recently required ISS training for all employees and has begun to develop training courses and education programs to support its ISS program. These courses are to be directed at all FAA employees or contractors who are system owners, developers, or risk assessors for any agency system. According to agency officials, all training courses will

---

[29]Computer Security Act of 1987, P.L. 100-235, Section 5(a).

reflect the agency's recently issued ISS policy and the planned supplemental directives that will outline how to implement the policy.

While these new efforts are promising, FAA needs to complete its efforts to issue the information security policy directives, and to develop and implement the new training courses. Until it does so, the agency will continue to operate at increased risk that its employees will not be knowledgeable about security rules as they perform their duties—thereby further risking critical information, systems, and resources.

FAA's Service Continuity Efforts Have Been Inadequate

Losing the capability to process, retrieve, and protect information maintained electronically can significantly affect an agency's ability to accomplish its mission. Service continuity controls ensure that, when unexpected events occur, critical operations continue without undue interruption and critical and sensitive data are protected. FAA's former and current information system security policies require that contingency plans be developed for all operational systems prior to system accreditation. Also, its physical security policy requires that contingency plans be completed for facilities.

FAA's efforts to develop these plans have been inadequate. The agency was unable to provide any system-specific contingency plans on its six accredited systems, and instead provided facility-specific contingency plans or maintenance handbooks. An FAA official stated that, while the agency does not currently have information system security contingency plans, it is in the process of creating guidance for contingency planning focused on information systems security needs. With regard to facility contingency plans, FAA facilities generally produce these plans, but, as noted earlier, FAA's own facilities' physical security assessment reports frequently cited these plans as inadequate. FAA officials noted that they plan to address these shortcomings as part of their efforts to accredit ATC facilities.

While these efforts are ongoing, FAA officials noted that the NAS is currently protected from a single point of failure because there is a significant amount of redundancy among ATC systems and facilities. They noted that there are primary and secondary systems and facilities, as well as manual procedures for backing key systems up. These redundancies often prove useful when a system's hardware fails or when weather or power outages affect a facility. FAA officials acknowledged that switching from a primary to a backup system or facility often results in delays, but stressed that they would not compromise aviation safety.

These redundancies have helped support the NAS to date, however, two FAA security officials acknowledged that the agency needs to develop system contingency plans and correct inadequacies in facility contingency plans. Other officials believe that the existing contingency plans are sufficient, but acknowledged that they have not yet assessed the effects of security breaches on all systems. FAA needs to assess the effects of security breaches on all systems, develop system-specific contingency plans to address potential security breaches, and correct inadequacies in its facility contingency plans. Until FAA does so, it lacks assurance that it is prepared to quickly and effectively recover from a variety of unanticipated disruptions.

FAA Has Not Fully Implemented An Effective Intrusion Detection Capability

Even strong controls may not block all intrusions and misuse, but organizations can reduce the risks associated with such events if they promptly take steps to detect and respond to such events before significant damage can be done. In addition, accounting for and analyzing security problems and incidents are effective ways for organizations to gain a better understanding of threats to their information and of the costs of their security-related problems. Such analyses can pinpoint vulnerabilities that need to be addressed to help ensure that they will not be exploited again. In this regard, problem and incident reports can provide valuable input for risk assessments, help in prioritizing security improvement efforts, and be used to illustrate risks and related trends in reports to senior management.

To detect and respond to intrusions on its systems, FAA recently established a Computer Security and Intrusion Response Capability (CSIRC). It has subsequently implemented 12 network intrusion detection devices to monitor network traffic and to help identify cyberthreats. Also, FAA's recently approved ISS policy requires all systems security incidents to be reported to the appropriate security officer and the CSIRC.

To detect and respond to intrusions at facilities, FAA's physical security policy requires incidents (e.g., arson, assault, bomb threats, vandalism) to be reported in a timely manner to identify the loss and damage to FAA property and facilities, as well as the frequency of adverse events which occur at facilities.

Page 25   GAO/T-AIMD-00-330 FAA Computer Security

FAA Has Not Yet Fully Implemented its CSIRC; Past Incidents Not Always Handled Quickly or Effectively

FAA has not yet fully implemented an effective intrusion detection capability that allows the agency to detect, analyze, and report computer security incidents in a timely fashion. According to FAA officials, the CSIRC will be fully operational in June 2001 and much remains to be done to achieve this goal. Specifically, FAA is currently installing the necessary equipment—phone lines, cable, desks, etc.—at one of its facilities, and needs to finalize and issue its draft CSIRC policies and procedures.

In the meantime, FAA's current CSIRC capabilities are limited in that they do not allow for a timely response and not all needed information is being captured. The CSIRC is staffed with contract employees who are responsible for monitoring data gathered by network intrusion detection devices and forwarding this data to the CIO's office for analysis. However, CSIRC staff do not provide 24-hour monitoring of the intrusion detection devices, and when they are on duty, there is a 4-hour delay between the recording of information captured by these devices, and the reporting of this information to the CIO's office for analysis and response. Also, the agency does not have a complete listing of all incidents that occur. According to FAA, additional network intrusion detection devices need to be installed at various sites to achieve full operational capability, and the various field offices have not always been rigorous in reporting incidents to the CIO's office.

In addition to limitations in its intrusion data gathering and response, FAA is also not effectively using intrusion data to prevent or minimize damage from future incidents by identifying patterns or trends. As noted above, once the information has been gathered from the intrusion detection devices, it is provided to the CIO office where a single analyst has been tasked with reviewing and analyzing the data, as well as reporting the results of all analysis to management. To date, only one such report has been provided to management and it only focused on specific incidents, not potential trends or patterns. CSIRC program officials stated that the CSIRC has not been a high priority until recently because of a lack of management commitment, as a result, there has been a lack of funding devoted to this activity.

FAA has also not been timely and effective in addressing selected incidents. To evaluate FAA's efforts in addressing incidents, we selected a sample of 10 incidents and reviewed the agency's resolution efforts.[30]

---

[30]We did not perform a statistically valid sample because FAA was unable to identify the universe of incidents. We judgmentally selected 10 incidents based on potential impact on NAS operations and whether the incident required an agencywide solution.

Based on our review, we concluded that the majority of these incidents were not detected in a timely manner and none of the vulnerabilities they revealed had been effectively corrected. For example, one system was initially compromised in August 1998 because default vendor settings had not been changed during system installation. However, FAA did not address this issue until May 1999. In another instance, a system that was being attacked was located at a contractor facility and the contractor failed to immediately notify FAA. Three months after being notified, FAA moved the system to an agency controlled environment and acknowledged the need to issue an agencywide policy addressing FAA systems located at other than agency facilities to prevent similar occurrences. However, the agency has not yet issued this policy.

While FAA has made progress, it needs to increase its efforts to establish a fully operational CSIRC that allows for the detection, analysis, and reporting of all incidents in a timely manner. Until it does so, FAA systems will remain vulnerable to potential attack and unable to respond quickly and effectively against threats.

Actions to Address Physical Security Incidents Appear Appropriate; But Not All Incidents Being Reported

FAA appears to be effectively addressing all known physical security incidents, however, the agency's facility assessments clearly show that all incidents are not being reported. During the period May 1, 1998, to April 14, 2000, 913 physical security incidents were reported at FAA facilities. However, because all incidents that occur within the agency's facilities are not being reported to security personnel, a complete list of incidents is unavailable. We selected 20 incidents that had been reported at critical facilities.[31] Based upon our review of these incidents, it appeared that timely and appropriate action had been taken by FAA to resolve the issues. The type of incidents ranged from suspicious packages, to unauthorized persons walking around FAA facilities, to a facility's failure to obtain clearances for foreign national visitors. In all instances, it appeared that FAA had taken appropriate action to resolve the incident, including contacting the proper authorities. In addition, for those incidents where the date and/or time were clear, they appeared to have been resolved in a timely manner.

Even though the incidents being reported have been effectively addressed, as previously noted, all physical security incidents are not being reported.

---

[31]We did not perform a statistically valid sample because FAA was unable to identify the universe of incidents. We judgmentally selected 20 incidents that occurred at facilities designated by the FAA as either security level (SL) 2, 3, or 4 with SL 4 being the most critical.

Page 27   GAO/T-AIMD-00-330 FAA Computer Security

Because all incidents are not being reported, FAA facilities still remain vulnerable, and in all likelihood, any unreported incidents are not being addressed by security or other agency personnel, thereby jeopardizing workplace safety. FAA needs to ensure that all physical security incidents are being reported.

In summary, FAA is making progress, but its computer security exposure is significant and pervasive with a lot of work remaining. FAA's efforts to prevent unauthorized access to data are inadequate in all critical areas we reviewed—personnel security, facility physical security, system access security, entitywide security program planning and management, and service continuity. FAA has often not yet developed the needed policies and procedures to implement an effective information security program. Where policies and procedures exist—in the areas of personnel and physical security—the agency is not in full compliance. FAA management needs to implement our prior recommendations and address the weaknesses raised in this statement. Until it does so, its critical assets—systems, facilities, information, people—will remain vulnerable to attack from both internal and external sources.

With the increase in attempted intrusions in recent years of various entities' systems by unauthorized users, the agency must also implement an effective intrusion detection capability for its critical computer systems and facilities. Until it does so, these assets will remain vulnerable to intruders who could potentially disrupt system operations or obtain access to sensitive information. In addition, FAA will continue to respond to security violations in an ad hoc manner or fail to respond at all. As a result, it will be poorly positioned to prevent, or to minimize, damage from future incidents.

Contacts and Acknowledgements

For information about this testimony, please contact Joel C. Willemssen at (202) 512-6408 or by e-mail at willemssenj.aimd@gao.gov. Individuals making key contributions to this testimony included Nabajyoti Barkakati, Phoebe Furey, David Hayes, Cynthia Jackson, Colleen Phillips, Tracy Pierson, Keith Rhodes, and Glenda Wright.

OBJECTIVES, SCOPE, AND METHODOLOGY

The objectives of our review were to identify (1) FAA's history of computer security weaknesses, (2) the adequacy of FAA's efforts to prevent unauthorized access to data and (3) the effectiveness of processes implemented by the agency for detecting, responding to, and reporting anomalies and computer misuse.

To identify FAA's history of computer security weaknesses, we summarized key findings and recommendations from our prior reports on FAA's computer security program in general and its personnel security program in particular.[32]

To evaluate the adequacy of FAA's efforts to prevent unauthorized access to data, we

- reviewed federal security requirements specified in the Computer Security Act of 1987 (Public Law 100-235), Paperwork Reduction Act of 1995 (Public Law 104-13), as amended, OMB Circular A-130, Appendix III, "Security of Federal Automated Information Systems," the 1996 Clinger-Cohen Act, An Introduction to Computer Security: The NIST Handbook, and the Presidential Decision Directive 63 White Paper to identify federal security requirements;

- evaluated relevant policies and procedures, including Order 1600.54B, FAA Automated Information Systems Security Handbook; Order 1370.82, Information Systems Security Program; Order 1600.1D, Personnel Security Program; Order 1600.69, FAA Facility Security Management Program; Order 1900.47A, Air Traffic Services Contingency Plan; Order 1900.1F, FAA Emergency Operations Plan; and Order 6100.1E, Maintenance of NAS En Route Stage A – Air Traffic Control System, to identify agency security requirements;

- analyzed key program documents, including FAA's Telecommunications Security Risk Management Plan, Information System Security Architecture, Draft NAS Risk Assessment, Volpe National Transportation Systems Center's *Preliminary Security Assessment of Air Traffic Services (ATS) Systems*, FAA's Critical Infrastructure Protection Plan and Critical Infrastructure Protection Remediation Plan to obtain an understanding of the agency's computer security program and any plans to improve the program;

---

[32]GAO/AIMD-98-155, May 18, 1998; GAO/AIMD-00-55, December 23, 1999; GAO/AIMD-00-169, May 31, 2000; GAO/AIMD-00-252, August 16, 2000.

Page 29   GAO/T-AIMD-00-330 FAA Computer Security

- analyzed reports from FAA's Consolidated Personnel Management Information System which contains investigation status information. Selected a statistically valid sample of 32 headquarters employees and reviewed their personnel and security folders to validate the reasonableness of the background searches performed based on the individual's job description;

- worked with an FAA security official to query the database containing information on contractor employees' background searches to determine whether the contractor employees who had worked on, or were working on, system vulnerability assessments met FAA requirements for background searches;

- analyzed data from FAA's Facility Security Reporting System (FSRS) to determine the assessment and accreditation status of all staffed ATC facilities under Order 1600.69;

- analyzed physical security assessment reports for all security level 2, 3, and 4 staffed ATC facilities to determine the degree of compliance;[33]

- analyzed security risk management assessments to identify additional facility security risks;

- analyzed security certification and authorization packages for ATC systems that have been certified and authorized (including systems granted interim authorizations) to determine adherence to policy;

- analyzed risk assessments for ATC systems and the results of FAA's penetration testing efforts, including documentation denoting the status of corrective actions identified to ascertain the extent of the NAS' vulnerability to internal and external intrusion;

- analyzed the technical specifications for three developmental ATC systems to determine if security requirements existed that were based on detailed assessments;[34] and

---

[33]ATC facilities include towers, terminal radar approach control facilities, en route centers, center approach control facilities, radar approach control facilities, flight service stations, and radar sites. Security level 4 facilities are most critical to national security and NAS operations. Security level 2 and 3 facilities are also essential to NAS operations but to a lesser degree.

[34]The three ATC systems selected were not intended to be a representative sample. FAA did not provide the complete universe of ATC systems under development until later in the review. Because of the timeframe for job completion, we were unable to wait for this information, therefore, we selected three systems from initial documentation provided by the agency.

- interviewed officials from the Offices of the Information Services/Chief Information Officer, Civil Aviation Security, Air Traffic Services, Human Resource Management, and Research and Acquisitions to determine responsibility for policy development, implementation, and enforcement. We also interviewed officials from FAA's William J. Hughes Technical Center.

We did not conduct independent testing of systems and facilities to validate the information reported by the agency.

To evaluate the effectiveness of processes implemented by the agency for detecting, responding to, and reporting anomalies and computer misuse, we

- evaluated relevant policies and procedures, including Order 1600.54B, FAA Automated Information Systems Security Handbook; Order 1370.82, Information Systems Security Program; Order 1600.69, FAA Facility Security Management Program; and draft Computer Security Incident Response Capability (CSIRC) planning documents to determine the extent of FAA's incident reporting and handling capability;

- analyzed incident data maintained by the agency and for a sample of incidents reviewed the resolution status to evaluate the agency's identification, resolution, and reporting of incidents;[35] and

- interviewed officials from the Offices of Information Services/Chief Information Officer, Civil Aviation Security, and Air Traffic Services to determine the extent to which FAA information security incidents are being detected, investigated, and reported.

In addition, we obtained comments on a draft of this testimony from FAA officials, including representatives from the offices of the Chief Information Officer, Associate Administrator for Civil Aviation Security, and the Associate Administrator for Research and Acquisition, and incorporated these comments as appropriate throughout the document. These officials generally agreed with our suggested actions to address identified weaknesses. We performed our work from March 2000 through September 2000 at FAA headquarters in Washington, D.C. and at the William J. Hughes Technical Center located in Atlantic City, NJ in accordance with generally accepted government auditing standards.

---

[35]Incident data was maintained for both systems and facilities. System-specific incident data covered the period May 1998 to early July 2000. Facility incident data covered the period May 1, 1998 to April 14, 2000.

Appendix I
OBJECTIVES, SCOPE, AND
METHODOLOGY

(511836)

GAO Contact and Staff Acknowledgments

GAO Contact

Colleen Phillips, (202) 512-6326

Acknowledgments

Individuals making key contributions to the testimony and this report included Nabajyoti Barkakati, Michael Fruitman, Phoebe Furey, David Hayes, Cynthia Jackson, Tracy Pierson, Keith Rhodes, and Glenda Wright.

Ordering Information

The first copy of each GAO report is free. Additional copies of reports are $2 each. A check or money order should be made out to the Superintendent of Documents. VISA and MasterCard credit cards are accepted, also.

Orders for 100 or more copies to be mailed to a single address are discounted 25 percent.

Orders by mail:
U.S. General Accounting Office
P.O. Box 37050
Washington, DC 20013

Orders by visiting:
Room 1100
700 4th St. NW (corner of 4th and G Sts. NW)
U.S. General Accounting Office
Washington, DC

Orders by phone:
(202) 512-6000
fax: (202) 512-6061
TDD (202) 512-2537

Each day, GAO issues a list of newly available reports and testimony. To receive facsimile copies of the daily list or any list from the past 30 days, please call (202) 512-6000 using a touchtone phone. A recorded menu will provide information on how to obtain these lists.

Orders by Internet:
For information on how to access GAO reports on the Internet, send an e-mail message with "info" in the body to:

info@www.gao.gov

or visit GAO's World Wide Web home page at:

http://www.gao.gov

To Report Fraud, Waste, or Abuse in Federal Programs

Contact one:

- Web site: http://www.gao.gov/fraudnet/fraudnet.htm
- e-mail: fraudnet@gao.gov
- 1-800-424-5454 (automated answering system)

PRINTED ON RECYCLED PAPER

United States
General Accounting Office
Washington, D.C. 20548-0001

Official Business
Penalty for Private Use $300

Address Correction Requested

www.ingramcontent.com/pod-product-compliance
Lightning Source LLC
Chambersburg PA
CBHW082114070326
40689CB00052B/4699